CONTENTS

ABOUT AUTHOR

Mark Lyndon-Jones

Mark Lyndon-Jones is a passionate and dedicated coach, consultant, pastor and specialist in the field of discipling men. With over 20 years of experience, Mark has honed his expertise in empowering men through the transformative process of discipleship.

Mark's primary focus is on guiding men on their spiritual journey through a holistic approach. He provides corporate and personalised coaching that help men navigate the challenges and triumphs of their faith walk.

Mark's approach combines deep biblical knowledge with practical application, enabling men to grow spiritually, develop strong character, and live out their faith in everyday life.

In addition to his coaching services, Mark also serves as a consultant for churches, particularly through MPower the National Men's Ministry of the Elim Churches, a specific ministry that he pioneered on behalf of the movement in 2014. Before that he pioneered a highly effective ministry for men in South Wales (UK) known as the 'Band of Brothers', which featured on ITV Wales.

His experience has reached beyond MPower through national organisations and churches looking to establish or enhance their men's discipleship ministries.

With keen insight and strategic thinking, Mark can advise on effective initiatives that engage and equip men to be strong leaders in their families, churches and businesses.

Mark's specialised knowledge and experience have earned him a reputation as a go-to specialist in the field of discipling men. His heart for serving Christian men shines through in his dedication to encouraging compassionate living against a backdrop of cultural toxic masculinity, balanced marriages, and intentional parenting.

If you are seeking transformation in your faith journey as a man, or if your church or organisation desires to strengthen its men's discipleship efforts, Mark Lyndon-Jones is the trusted and knowledgeable resource you need. Together, let's empower men to become all that God has called them to be.

Mark has also featured on Christian Radio & Online Digital platforms and is a public speaker both home and abroad. He has led teams of men on missions to Europe and Africa even to the Democratic Republic of Congo. He engages hundreds of men each week through his Empowered: Fuel for the Week Devotional.

Adventure is never too far away with Mark and his ministry to men.

Mark has been married to Gail for nearly 40 years and together they have raised four sons to successful adulthood and enjoy the blessings of grandchildren and a growing family. Mark is also the senior Pastor of the Elim Church in Porth, South Wales.

DEDICATION

To the incredible band of brothers who have journeyed with me in life, both past and present, and those who will continue to stand together in the future. Your unwavering support, camaraderie, and shared experiences have helped shaped me into the person and leader I am today. Through the highs and lows, triumphs, and challenges, you have been a constant source of strength and inspiration. This dedication is a testament to an unbreakable bond in Christ. Thank you. Your Friend & Brother MLJ

PREFACE

Mark and I met in our 20's at Kensington Temple in London where he was leading the worship ministry in a group of 20 somethings at a time when God was moving powerfully. He encouraged me to join the worship team and then, some years later when he and his wife Gail left London, he tagged me to lead the worship ministry.

Years later he moved to Wales and joined the church I was leading in Cardiff and a new adventure began. Starting in the front window of a café where Mark and a few guys were meeting without their wives at the end of a small group series which he had been leading, Mark opened the Bible and just started sharing, as he does.

Out of that small beginning came an initiative and a journey that led to the Band of Brothers ministry that reached a whole bunch of men across the city of Cardiff and beyond for Jesus.

Many of those guys just didn't really have it in them to come near the regular church services, but over time, as Mark opened the Bible with hundreds and hundreds of men, sometimes in a coffee shop, sometimes in a church building, often in the most random and unbelievable places, he began to see a way to inspire men to reach other men for Jesus, and to find out how to do life together.

They came with their questions and doubts but were drawn to the compelling person of Jesus. They began to ask not just is He real and true, but how do we do follow Him through all the stuff that all of us have to deal with, our fears and our uncertainty, our passion and our many failures and disappointments. How do we do life "with Him."

You might get from what I'm saying that Mark is a passionate guy. He has a creative and courageous faith, believing that God uses us in ways that often we haven't yet dared to believe

This Study comes out of the years of journey with men. Now a local church Pastor in the Rhondda Valley and National Leader of Elim's MPower Men's Ministry, Mark has written this book to help men disciple men.

It's rooted in the book of Nehemiah in the Word of God and Mark shares here principles which have become the values behind the men's ministry that he leads. But it's more than a study guide. At its heart is a principle that men can reach and lead other men and encourage them to have the same passion for doing life for Jesus.

I know this book will be a blessing to many and encourage many men to go on a fresh journey. I pray the values that underpin the kind of ministry that Mark is so rightly invested in will be deeply sown into the lives of many guys as a result.

I believe that God still comes to real guys in real places going through real stuff. He comes like He always has to call them into a transformational life, where He takes the things that He has already put within us and shapes us into His new creation people. Let this study strengthen you and the guys you do life with.

Chris Cartwright

General Superintendent,

Elim Pentecostal Churches.

WHAT MEN'S GROUP FACILITATORS AND PRACTITIONERS ARE SAYING

Mark Lyndon Jones thunders a message of conviction and character to men throughout the UK and beyond. With conviction he relentlessly speaks into so many men's lives, he is a man of God who has been commissioned to build men to reach their true potential within this generation. This man is a real representation of God's prophetic voice in this nation in men's ministry.

Alistair Whitmoor-Pryer - Kingdom Entrepreneur

Mark Lyndon-Jones has been leading ministry to men for many years, he has a heart to see men engage with the Bible, on both a spiritual and practical level. He is a great listener and facilitator of men's ministry, a man of prayer and the Word. He has a heart to see men discipled and go deeper in their personal journey with the Lord.

John Barwell - Band of Brothers

My personal experience of Mark Lyndon-Jones has been a resolute and impactful leader in men's ministry for two decades. His commitment to helping men connect with the Bible on a spiritual and practical level is truly commendable. He has been a personal mentor and inspiration to me since 2009. He creates spaces where men feel valued and encouraged to walk deeper in their faith journey.

Simon Mitchell - Band of Brothers and Porth Elim Church

Mark Lyndon-Jones's ministry to men stands out as a beacon of strength and inspiration. His experience in leading men's ministry has equipped him with the tools to effectively engage others with the Bible both spiritually and practically. Through his genuine care, unwavering commitment to prayer, and rich understanding of the Word, Mark empowers men to deepen their connection with God and supports them in their journey towards becoming compassionate leaders in life, marriage, and parenting.

Carl Long - MPower Men's Events

Mark is on a spiritual mission to disciple men of all walks of life; reconnecting them to their God given role in society. If you need no nonsense spirit-filled content, full of meat, to hold you accountable. Look no further, welcome home.

Roy McEwen (Solutions Architect & Entrepenuer)

HOW TO USE THIS MANUAL

Nehemiah's Strategic Approach - 'For Men & Men who Lead Men' is one of a series of practical and tactical resources tailored specifically as a blueprint for discipling men who are seeking guidance, inspiration, and practical steps for living out their faith in a meaningful way.

This manual is designed to function as a guide for men's discussion groups and a personal workbook for navigating life strategically and prayerfully.

By following the structure and using the various resources provided, you will be equipped to make the most of this valuable resource personally and in your Men's Group.

Throughout this manual, several key themes will be explored, including strategic mindset, prayerful dependence, visionary leadership, persistent diligence, community restoration, and remarkable success. Each chapter will delve into these themes, offering insights and strategies for personal and ministry development.

At the beginning of each chapter, you will find key verses that anchor the content and provide a biblical foundation. These verses will help you connect with God's Word and apply it to your life and ministry.

For example, in Chapter 2: "A Strategic Heart and Mindset" - We will explore the importance of developing a strategic mindset. The four key aspects include Confidentiality and Observation; Assessment and Strategy Development; Rationale and Persuasion; Preparation and Resource Management.

At the end of each chapter, there are discussion questions provided for reflection and further exploration. Engage with these questions either individually or as a men's group, fostering meaningful discussions and deeper understanding.

To support your personal spiritual growth, devotional thoughts are included after each chapter. These can serve as a source of inspiration and guidance as you seek to apply the principles discussed. Additionally, leverage social media platforms to engage with others, share insights, and foster a sense of community around the material covered.

By following the chapter structure, engaging with the discussion questions, reflecting on the devotional thoughts, and utilising social media platforms as a means of community engagement, you will maximise the benefits of this manual. May it serve as a valuable resource in your personal growth, ministry journey and Men's Groups.

KEY THEMES

1. Prayerful Dependence: Nehemiah's reliance on prayer highlights the need for men to seek God's guidance and wisdom in all aspects of life.
2. The Strategic Mindset: Nehemiah demonstrates his strategic mindset in assessing the situation and planning for the task at hand.
3. Visionary Leadership: Nehemiah exemplifies the importance of setting goals, rallying others, and leading with integrity.
4. Persistent Diligence: Despite challenges and opposition, Nehemiah shows the value of staying focused, putting in the demanding work, and not giving up.
5. Community Restoration: Nehemiah prioritises rebuilding the city walls, emphasising the significance of investing in one's family, church, and local community.
6. Remarkable Success: Nehemiah's remarkable achievement was the completion of the wall in Jerusalem, a task accomplished in just fifty-two days, highlighting his leadership, determination, and the Favor of God.

CHAPTER 1
NEHEMIAH'S PRAYERFUL DEPENDENCE

INTRODUCTION

As Christian men navigating the challenges of everyday life, we can draw inspiration from the resolute prayerful dependence displayed by Nehemiah. In just four key points, we will explore the essence of his unwavering faith and discover how it can guide our own journey.

KEY VERSES

"When I heard these things, I sat down and wept. For some days I mourned and fasted and prayed before the God of heaven. Then I said: 'Lord, the God of heaven, the great and awesome God, who keeps his covenant of love with those who love him and keep his commandments, let your ear be attentive and your eyes open to hear the prayer your servant is praying before you day and night for your servants, the people of Israel" (Nehemiah 1:4-6).

1. GENUINE GRIEF

Nehemiah's heartfelt response to the ruins of Jerusalem goes beyond mere emotions—it fuels transformative action. Through his authentic sorrow, he channels his passion into rebuilding and restoring what is broken. This lesson teaches us that acknowledging and engaging with the brokenness around us can motivate meaningful change.

2. INTENTIONAL DISCIPLINES

By embracing intentional disciplines such as fasting, mourning, and prayer, Nehemiah demonstrates his humble reliance on God's strength and guidance. These deliberate acts deepen our connection with the Divine, empowering us to face life's trials. Just as a rigorous training regimen prepares an action hero for battle, these disciplines equip Christian men for spiritual warfare.

3. REVERENCE FOR GOD

In Nehemiah's prayer, he reverently recognizes God's greatness—the awe-inspiring One who holds all power and authority. By acknowledging God's majesty, we align ourselves with His purposes and tap into His limitless strength. Cultivating a deep sense of reverence positions us to experience God's provision and walk confidently in His will.

4. PERSISTENT INTERCESSION

Nehemiah's unrelenting intercession on behalf of Israel exemplifies the power of persistent prayer. He fervently lifts up the needs of others, seeking divine favour and intervention. This committed approach mirrors the unwavering pursuit of an action hero fighting against all odds to rescue those in need. Christian men are called to emulate Nehemiah's tenacity through consistent intercession, advocating for others before the throne of grace.

CONCLUSION

Nehemiah's unwavering prayerful dependence provides a blueprint for Christian men seeking to navigate the complexities of life. By embracing genuine grief, intentional disciplines, reverence for God, and persistent intercession, we can cultivate a resilient faith that empowers us to bring about positive change in our spheres of influence. Let us heed the call to be modern-day Nehemiah's—heroes who rely on God's strength, wisdom, and compassion to impact our families, communities, and the world around us.

DISCUSSION QUESTIONS

1. How can we apply Nehemiah's grief in our lives today? How can we channel our passion into meaningful action?

2. Discuss the intentional disciplines modelled by Nehemiah. How do they deepen our connection with God?

3. How can we cultivate reverence for God in our daily lives?

4. How can we develop a lifestyle of persistent prayer and advocacy for others?

NOTES

____

____

____

____

____

____

____

MLJ'S DEVOTIONAL ON NEHEMIAH 1:4

PASSAGE

Nehemiah 1:4 NIV - "When I heard these things, I sat down and wept. For some days I mourned and fasted and prayed before the God of heaven."

PERSPECTIVE

Genuine grief moves us to action. It stirs our desire for change and restoration.

POINT

Acknowledge the brokenness around you and let it fuel your passion for making a difference.

PONDER

Reflect on what breaks your heart and use it as motivation to transform lives.

PRAY

Dear God, help us feel genuine grief that leads to action. Guide us in making a positive impact. Amen.

SOCIAL MEDIA POSTS

POST 1

🙏 Seeking God's guidance in prayer, just as Nehemiah did in Nehemiah 1:4. Let us approach Him with humility and seek His strength! @REVxMLJ #PrayerfulSeeking #Nehemiah104

POST 2

Reflecting on Nehemiah's example of fervent prayer in Nehemiah 1:4. Let us embrace the power of prayer to overcome challenges and seek God's wisdom! @REVxMLJ #PowerOfPrayer #Nehemiah104

POST 3

🙌 Inspired by Nehemiah's prayerful dependence on God in Nehemiah 1:4. May we trust in His provision and find strength in Him alone! @REVxMLJ #DependOnGod #Nehemiah104

CHAPTER 2
THE STRATEGIC HEART AND MINDSET

INTRODUCTION

Nehemiah demonstrates his strategic mindset in assessing the situation and planning for the task at hand.

KEY VERSES

"I set out during the night with a few others. I had not told anyone what my God had put in my heart to do for Jerusalem. There were no mounts with me except the one I was riding on..." (Nehemiah 2:11-16).

1. CONFIDENTIALITY AND OBSERVATION

Nehemiah initially keeps his mission to rebuild the walls of Jerusalem confidential, without sharing it with anyone. He personally inspects the condition of the walls during the night, gaining first-hand knowledge of the extent of the damage.

2. ASSESSMENT AND STRATEGY DEVELOPMENT

Nehemiah examines the broken walls, destroyed gates, and fallen debris, taking note of the specific areas that require attention. This thorough assessment helps him formulate a clear plan for the rebuilding process.

3. RATIONALE AND PERSUASION

After completing his assessment, Nehemiah gathers the necessary information before presenting his case to the officials, leaders, and people of Jerusalem. He articulates the purpose behind the project and emphasises God's favour on their endeavour, inspiring their support and cooperation.

4. PREPARATION AND RESOURCE MANAGEMENT

Nehemiah goes beyond presenting a compelling vision; he outlines practical steps needed for the successful implementation of the rebuilding process. He prepares a detailed plan, gathers resources, and ensures proper allocation and distribution of materials.

CONCLUSION

Nehemiah's actions in Chapter 2 demonstrate his strategic thinking and careful planning. By operating with secrecy, conducting thorough assessments, persuasively communicating his vision, and managing resources effectively, Nehemiah sets the stage for the successful execution of the rebuilding project. His strategic approach serves as an inspiration for Christian men seeking to be intentional and forward-thinking in their faith walk.

DISCUSSION QUESTIONS

1. In what ways can Nehemiah's choice to keep his mission confidential inspire us/me/men to demonstrate effective leadership in our personal lives?

2. How can Nehemiah's assessment of the damaged walls encourage us to reflect on and rebuild areas of own lives that broken or in need of improvement?

3. How does Nehemiah's emphasis on persuasive communication and reliance on God's favour resonate with ours, and how does it inspire us to seek support and guidance in our personal journeys?

4. How can Nehemiah's focus on preparation and resource management inspire us to be intentional and proactive in preparing ourselves for success in various areas of our lives?

NOTES

MLJ'S DEVOTIONAL ON NEHEMIAH 2:11-16

PASSAGE

"I went to Jerusalem, and after staying there three days I set out during the night with a few others. I had not told anyone what my God had put in my heart to do for Jerusalem..."

PERSPECTIVE

Witness Nehemiah's commitment to rebuilding Jerusalem's walls with stealth, determination, and attention to detail. His example teaches Christian men the need for strategic planning and execution in the faith journey.

POINT

As Christian men, purpose and intentionality guide our actions. Like Nehemiah, we must assess areas needing rebuilding, be it relationships, spirituality, or personal struggles. Adopt a strategic mindset to initiate necessary changes.

PONDER

Reflect on your life. Identify areas in need of rebuilding. Seek God's guidance for a strategic approach. Embrace secrecy, observation, assessment, and preparation in your endeavors.

PRAY

Heavenly Father, grant wisdom as I rebuild and strengthen my life. Guide me strategically, with perseverance and diligence for needed changes. May my actions align with Your will and bring You glory. Amen.

SOCIAL MEDIA POSTS

POST 1

📖 Discover the leadership lessons from Nehemiah's strategy! Keep your mission confidential, assess diligently, and inspire others. #LeadershipLessons #REVxMLJ 🙌

POST 2

🦉 Reflect on Nehemiah's approach to rebuilding and apply it to your personal life. Assess, communicate persuasively, and rely on God's favour. 🏗️ 💪 @REVxMLJ #PersonalGrowth

POST 3

🛠️ 🚀 Learn from Nehemiah's resource management skills for success in life! Prepare, manage wisely, and rebuild with determination. @REVxMLJ #SuccessSkills.

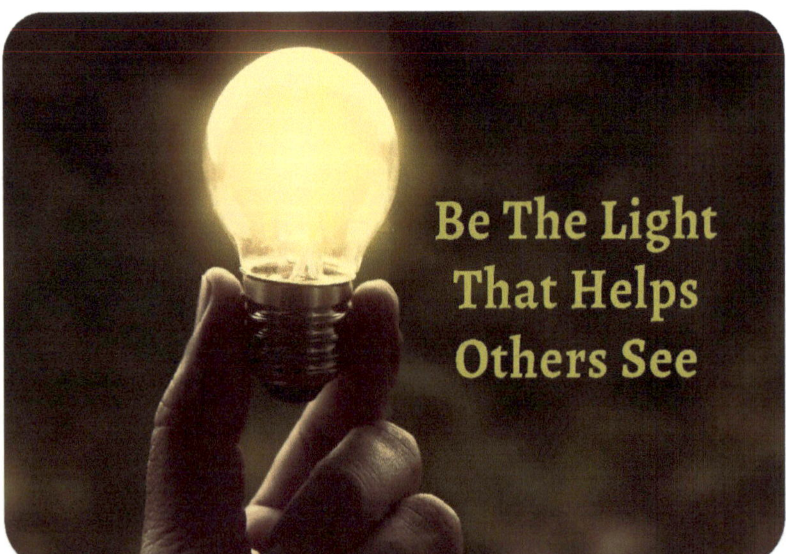

CHAPTER 3

VISIONARY LEADERSHIP

INTRODUCTION

Nehemiah's visionary leadership in the Bible serves as a timeless example of how a determined leader can inspire transformation and unity. Through his clear vision, effective communication, strategic planning, and unwavering faith, Nehemiah successfully rallied the people to rebuild the walls of Jerusalem.

KEY VERSES

"Then I said to them, 'You see the trouble we are in: Jerusalem lies in ruins, and its gates have been burned with fire. Come, let us rebuild the wall of Jerusalem, and we will no longer be in disgrace.' I also told them about the gracious hand of my God on me and what the king had said to me. They replied, 'Let us start rebuilding.' So, they began this good work" (Nehemiah 2:17-18).

1.CLEAR VISION

At a crucial moment when Jerusalem lay in ruins, Nehemiah articulated a powerful vision to restore the city's walls. His transparent acknowledgment of the current state created a sense of urgency. By presenting a clear solution and outlining the benefits of re-building, he inspired hope and motivated the people to action. Nehemiah's vision provided a collective purpose that united a fragmented community.

2. EFFECTIVE COMMUNICATION

Nehemiah skillfully communicated both his personal experiences and God's favor upon him to inspire trust and confidence in his followers. By sharing his encounters with the king and emphasising Divine assistance, he instilled faith in the hearts of the people. Nehemiah's authentic and persuasive communication style helped build rapport and encouraged active participation.

3. STRATEGIC PLANNING

Nehemiah's visionary leadership extended beyond inspiration; he developed a strategic plan to accomplish the daunting task of rebuilding the walls. By organising different groups to work on specific sections and addressing challenges strategically, Nehemiah maximised efficiency.

His meticulous planning enabled progress while maintaining a focus on quality and safety, ensuring the successful completion of the project.

4: UNWAVERING FAITH

Throughout the process, Nehemiah consistently demonstrated unwavering faith in God's provision and guidance. Despite opposition, he refused to be deterred or intimidated. Nehemiah relied on prayer and sought God's wisdom when making decisions. This unwavering faith not only strengthened his own resolve but also served as an inspiration to those around him, fueling their dedication and perseverance.

CONCLUSION

Nehemiah's visionary leadership exemplifies the transformative power of a clear vision, effective communication, strategic planning, and unwavering faith in inspiring unity and accomplishing extraordinary tasks.

DISCUSSION QUESTIONS

1. How can Nehemiah's clear vision of rebuilding the walls of Jerusalem inspire us to develop a clear vision for our own lives or projects? What steps can we take to articulate and communicate our vision effectively?
2. Nehemiah's effective communication played a crucial role in rallying people to join him in the rebuilding effort. How can we improve our communication skills to inspire and motivate others towards a shared goal?
3. Nehemiah's strategic planning ensured the successful completion of the project despite obstacles and opposition. In what ways can we apply strategic planning in our own endeavours to overcome challenges and achieve our desired outcomes?

NOTES

____

____

____

____

____

____

____

MLJ'S DEVOTIONAL ON NEHEMIAH 2:17-18

PASSAGE

"Then I said to them, 'You see the trouble we are in: Jerusalem lies in ruins, and its gates have been burned with fire. Come, let us rebuild the wall of Jerusalem, and we will no longer be in disgrace.' I also told them about the gracious hand of my God on me and what the king had said to me. They replied, 'Let us start rebuilding.' So they began this good work" (Nehemiah 2:17-18).

PERSPECTIVE

Just as Nehemiah saw the state of Jerusalem and took action, we too face challenges and hardships in our lives. But through God's guidance and provision, we can overcome any obstacle.

POINT

Let us not be discouraged by the ruins around us, but instead, let our faith in God fuel our determination to re-build. He is with us, empowering us with His strength and favor. We have the opportunity to turn disgrace into glory through our actions and reliance on Him.

PONDER

What areas in my life need re-building? How can I rely on God's guidance and provision to begin the process of restoration? Am I willing to take that first step?

PRAY

Heavenly Father, help me see the areas in my life that need re-building. Grant me the strength, wisdom, and perseverance to carry out this good work. Guide every endeavour, knowing that I can rely on Your gracious hand to lead me. In Jesus' name, amen.

SOCIAL MEDIA POSTS

POST 1

🙏 🔨 Rebuilding with Faith: Just as Nehemiah overcame challenges, we too can re-build what's broken. Let God guide our steps and turn disgrace into glory. #Faith #Restoration @REVxMLJ 🧱

POST 2

🚧 👷 Rise Above Ruins: Like Nehemiah, we face obstacles, but with God's provision, we can re-build and transform our lives. Let's start the good work today! 💪 ✨ @REVxMLJ #TransformationTuesday

POST 3

👀 🔑 Unlock Your Potential: Nehemiah's unwavering faith ignited change. Embrace the call to re-build areas of your life, trusting in God's guidance and favour. You can conquer anything! @REVxMLJ 🌟 💪 #MondayMotivation

CHAPTER 4

PERSISTENT DILIGENCE

INTRODUCTION

In the book of Nehemiah, we find a remarkable example of persistent diligence in the face of adversity. Nehemiah, a faithful servant of God, was entrusted with the task of rebuilding the walls of Jerusalem. Despite encountering numerous challenges and fierce opposition, he remained steadfast in his determination to fulfil God's purpose.

KEY VERSES

"So, we rebuilt the wall till all of it reached half its height, for the people worked with all their heart" (Nehemiah 4:6).

1. RECOGNIZING THE CHALLENGES

Nehemiah's journey was not without its hurdles. He encountered mocking, ridicule, and even threats from his enemies. The magnitude of the task ahead seemed overwhelming, with a broken-down wall that required significant effort to rebuild. Yet Nehemiah did not let these challenges discourage him. Instead, he acknowledged them and trusted in God's strength to overcome every obstacle.

2. UNWAVERING FOCUS

Amidst the adversity, Nehemiah maintained an unwavering focus on the task at hand. In Nehemiah 4:6, we read that he and his fellow workers had a relentless commitment to the work, stating, "For the people had a mind to work." Even when faced with distractions or schemes designed to hinder their progress, they did not waver from their purpose but remained dedicated to rebuilding Jerusalem's walls.

3. TRUSTING IN GOD'S PROVISION

Nehemiah understood that success was not solely dependent on his own efforts but on God's divine intervention. He sought the Lord through prayer and leaned on Him for guidance and protection. In difficult times, Nehemiah fervently relied on God's promise and provision, which enabled him to persevere with patience, trusting that God would see them through to the fulfilment of the work.

4. INSPIRING ENDURANCE AND RESULTS

Nehemiah's persistent diligence serves as an inspiration for us today. His unwavering commitment, focus, and trust in God led to the rebuilding of the walls of Jerusalem within a remarkable 52 days. The successful completion of this monumental task was not only a testament to Nehemiah's leadership but also a demonstration of God's faithfulness.

This story encourages us to persevere in the face of difficulties, believing that with God's help, we too can overcome obstacles and achieve great things.

CONCLUSION

Nehemiah's example teaches us the importance of staying focused and persistent, even in the midst of challenges and opposition. By acknowledging the hurdles, maintaining unwavering dedication, trusting in God's provision, and finding inspiration in Nehemiah's story, we can cultivate our own persistent diligence and experience success in our endeavours.

DISCUSSION QUESTIONS

1. How can we draw inspiration from Nehemiah's persistent diligence in our own lives? Can you think of any specific challenges or goals where applying this principle could make a difference?
2. In what ways do you see parallel situations in your life where opposition or setbacks may threaten to derail your determination? How can you apply Nehemiah's example to stay focused and persevere in those situations?
3. Reflecting on Nehemiah's reliance on God's provision and the power of prayer, how can we incorporate these principles into our own lives when facing challenges? Have you experienced moments where prayer and trust in God's guidance have helped you overcome obstacles?
4. Nehemiah's story highlights the importance of having a clear sense of purpose and unwavering commitment. How can we identify our own goals or tasks that require persistent diligence, and what steps can we take to maintain focus and dedication throughout the journey?

NOTES

As you discuss Nehemiah's persistent diligence, consider drawing personal parallels by sharing examples from your own experiences or challenges that resonate with the themes and lessons from Nehemiah's story. This will help relate the discussions to real-life circumstances and foster deeper connections to the concepts discussed.

MLJ'S DEVOTIONAL ON NEHEMIAH 4:6

PASSAGE

"So we built the wall, and all the wall was joined together to half its height, for the people had a mind to work."

PERSPECTIVE

In life, there will always be obstacles, opposition, and challenges that threaten our progress. Nehemiah faced ridicule and threats as he rebuilt Jerusalem's wall. But what set him apart was his unwavering determination and focus.

POINT

As Christian men, we are called to approach our lives with the same resolute mindset. Let us have a mind to work, unwavering in our commitment to what God has entrusted to us. Regardless of the hurdles before us, let us press forward with purpose and diligence.

PONDER

What challenges or opposition are holding you back from fulfilling God's purposes in your life? How can you develop a "mind to work" attitude and overcome these obstacles?

PRAY

Lord, grant me the strength and perseverance to face every challenge that comes my way. Help me maintain an unwavering focus on the tasks You have set before me. Grant me the courage to overcome opposition and press on with determination. In Jesus' name, amen.

SOCIAL MEDIA POSTS

POST 1

🙏 As Christian men, let's embrace Nehemiah's determination and have a "mind to work" attitude in fulfilling God's purposes! @REVxMLJ 💪 #MondayDevotional

POST 2

⚒️ Facing opposition or challenges? Remember Nehemiah's resilience in rebuilding the wall! Stay focused and press on towards your goals. @REVxMLJ 🧱 #StayDetermined

POST 3

🙌 Let's pray for strength and a steadfast mindset like Nehemiah! Nothing can stop us when we have a resolute commitment to God's calling. @REVxMLJ 🙏 #FaithfulMen

CHAPTER 5

COMMUNITY RESTORATION

INTRODUCTION

Nehemiah prioritises rebuilding the city walls, emphasising the significance of investing in one's family, church, and local community.

KEY VERSES

"I answered them by saying, 'The God of heaven will give us success. We his servants will start rebuilding, but as for you, you have no share in Jerusalem or any claim or historic right to it" (Nehemiah 2:20).

1. A VISION FOR RESTORATION

Nehemiah's deep sense of responsibility compelled him to take action. He recognized that a thriving community required strong foundations, both physically and spiritually. By prioritising the rebuilding of the city walls, he sent a clear message that investing in one's community is crucial. Nehemiah's vision serves as a reminder to us today, highlighting the importance of identifying areas in our own communities that require restoration.

2. THE POWER OF UNITY

Nehemiah's call to rebuild the walls did not fall on deaf ears. People from various backgrounds and professions came together, united in the common goal of restoring their community. This collective effort showcases the power of unity in bringing about positive change. It serves as a reminder that when we work together for a common cause, we can accomplish great things.

3. FAITH IN GOD'S PROVISION

Throughout his journey, Nehemiah displayed unwavering faith in God's provision. In Nehemiah 2:20, he confidently states that success would come from God, firmly rejecting any interference from those who opposed the rebuilding efforts. This bold declaration reminds us to trust in God's guidance and rely on His provision when seeking to restore and transform our own communities.

4. INVESTING IN FAMILY, CHURCH, AND COMMUNITY

Nehemiah understood the interconnectedness between family, church, and community. Through the rebuilding process, he worked tirelessly to strengthen these bonds. He encouraged families to work side-by-side, fostering a sense of unity and shared purpose.

Nehemiah's example reminds us of the importance of investing in our families, actively participating in our local church communities, and working towards the betterment of our wider society.

CONCLUSION

In a world where division and apathy can easily take hold, Nehemiah's story serves as an inspiration. It challenges us to actively engage in community restoration by identifying areas of need, fostering unity, having faith in God's provision, and investing in the well-being of our families, churches, and local communities. As we follow Nehemiah's example, we can become agents of positive change and bring about lasting transformation.

DISCUSSION QUESTIONS

1. How can we identify areas in our own communities that require restoration, and what steps can we take to address these needs?
2. In what ways can unity within a community contribute to successful restoration efforts? How can we foster unity among different groups and individuals with diverse backgrounds and interests?
3. Nehemiah demonstrated unwavering faith in God's provision throughout his journey. How can we cultivate a similar reliance on God when seeking to restore our communities? How can faith in God's guidance impact our approach to community restoration?
4. Nehemiah emphasised the importance of investing in family, church, and community. How can we apply this principle to our own lives? What specific actions can we take to strengthen the bonds within our families, actively engage in our local churches, and contribute to the betterment of our broader society?

NOTES

By discussing these questions and reflecting on Nehemiah's strategy for community restoration, we can gain valuable insights on how to effectively engage in the restoration and transformation of our own communities. It allows us to explore practical ways to identify needs, foster unity, rely on God's provision, and invest in the well-being of our families, churches, and local communities. Ultimately, these discussions can inspire us to take action and become agents of positive change in the places where we live and serve.

MLJ'S DEVOTIONAL ON NEHEMIAH 2:20

PASSAGE

I answered them by saying, 'The God of heaven will give us success. We his servants will start rebuilding, but as for you, you have no share in Jerusalem or any claim or historic right to it.

PERSPECTIVE

As Christian men, we face opposition in various forms when we seek to restore and rebuild our communities. Nehemiah's response to those who opposed the restoration of Jerusalem reminds us of the unwavering confidence we can have in God's provision and guidance.

POINT

When God calls us to engage in meaningful work, He equips us with the tools necessary for success. Our authority to rebuild comes from Him alone, and we must not be deterred by the naysayers or those who seek to hinder our progress.

PONDER

What opposition are you currently facing in your pursuit of community restoration? How can you rely on God's strength and authority to overcome these challenges?

PRAY

Heavenly Father, grant us the confidence and perseverance to withstand opposition as we strive to restore our communities. Help us trust in Your provision and guidance, knowing that our authority comes from You. Give us clarity and wisdom as we navigate the obstacles we encounter. In Jesus' name, we pray. Amen.

SOCIAL MEDIA POSTS

POST 1

🙏 As Christian men, let's be unshakable in our conviction to rebuild and restore our communities. With God's guidance, success is certain! @REVxMLJ #CommunityRestoration #ChristianMen

POST 2

🚧 Opposition may arise, but it won't stop us from fulfilling our calling as men of faith. Together, we can make a lasting impact on our communities! @REVxMLJ 💪 🌍 #MakeADifference #ChristianMen

POST 3

In the face of challenges, remember Nehemiah's example: rely on God's provision, trust His authority, and persist in restoring what's broken. @REVxMLJ

🛠️ Let's be men who bring hope and transformation!

#BeAnAgentOfChange #ChristianMen

CHAPTER 6
REMARKABLE SUCCESS

INTRODUCTION

Nehemiah's remarkable achievement was the completion of the wall in Jerusalem, a task accomplished in just fifty-two days, showcasing his leadership, determination, and the favour of God.

KEY VERSES

"So, the wall was completed on the twenty-fifth of Elul, in fifty-two days" (Nehemiah 6:15).

1: LEADERSHIP AND VISION

Nehemiah's success in rebuilding the walls of Jerusalem can be attributed to his exceptional leadership and vision. He effectively inspired and mobilised the people, rallying them around a common goal. His clear direction and meticulous planning ensured that everyone understood their roles and tasks, resulting in efficient progress.

2: DETERMINATION AND PERSEVERANCE

Nehemiah faced numerous challenges and opposition throughout the construction process. However, he demonstrated unwavering determination and perseverance, refusing to be discouraged or deterred by adversity. His resolute spirit served as an example for those working alongside him, encouraging them to press forward in the face of obstacles.

3: DIVINE FAVOUR AND GUIDANCE

Nehemiah's conviction that the God of heaven would provide success was not in vain. Throughout the project, God's favour and guidance were evident. Nehemiah's faith in God's provision allowed him to navigate difficult situations with wisdom and discernment. It was through this divine intervention that the construction progressed swiftly and flawlessly.

4: UNITY AND COLLABORATION

The remarkable success of rebuilding the walls in just fifty-two days can be attributed to the unity and collaboration among the people of Jerusalem. Everyone joined hands together, working diligently towards the common purpose. The spirit of cooperation, mutual support, and shared responsibility played a crucial role in overcoming challenges and achieving their extraordinary goal.

CONCLUSION

Nehemiah's remarkable success in rebuilding the walls of Jerusalem is a testament to his outstanding leadership, unwavering determination, reliance on divine favour, and the power of unity.

It teaches us valuable lessons on effective leadership, resilience in the face of adversity, trust in God's provision, and the significance of working together towards a shared vision. As we embark on our own endeavours, let Nehemiah's example inspire us to lead with purpose, remain steadfast, rely on God's guidance, and foster a spirit of collaboration.

DISCUSSION QUESTIONS

1. How can we apply Nehemiah's leadership and vision in our own lives? Can you think of any situations where clear direction and meticulous planning can lead to remarkable success?
2. Nehemiah showed great determination and perseverance throughout the rebuilding process. How can we cultivate this same level of resilience in our own endeavours? What strategies or mindset shifts can help us overcome obstacles and stay focused on our goals?
3. Nehemiah believed in the favour and guidance of God in achieving success. How can we rely on our faith or personal beliefs to navigate challenges and seek divine intervention in our own pursuits? Are there any specific practices or habits that can help strengthen our trust in a higher power?
4. The success of rebuilding the walls in Jerusalem was made possible through unity and collaboration among the people. How can we foster a similar spirit of teamwork in our own projects or communities? What steps can we take to encourage mutual support, shared responsibility, and a sense of common purpose among those we work with?

NOTES

By exploring and discussing these questions, we can gain insights into how Nehemiah's remarkable success relates to our own lives. We can draw inspiration from his leadership qualities, learn from his determination, reflect on the role of faith in achieving our goals, and consider the power of collaboration for accomplishing remarkable feats.

MLJ'S DEVOTIONAL ON NEHEMIAH 2:20

PASSAGE

"So I answered them and said to them, 'The God of heaven Himself will prosper us; therefore we His servants will arise and build, but you have no heritage or right or memorial in Jerusalem.'"

PERSPECTIVE

Nehemiah's unwavering faith in God's provision allowed him to conquer seemingly insurmountable challenges. He stood firm against doubters and adversaries, trusting in the power of the Almighty.

POINT

As Christian men, we are called to emulate Nehemiah's determination and resilience. Our trust in God's favor and guidance can propel us towards remarkable success, even amidst adversity.

PONDER

Reflect on the times when doubts and opposition arise in your life. How can you strengthen your faith and trust in God's provision? How might standing firm inspire those around you?

PRAY

Dear Lord, grant us unwavering faith and courage to rise above obstacles. Help us remember that with You, all things are possible. Guide us as we strive for remarkable success, shining Your light in every facet of our lives. In Jesus' name, amen.

SOCIAL MEDIA POSTS

POST 1

🙏 Trusting in God's provision leads to remarkable success. Let Nehemiah's unwavering faith inspire you to overcome challenges and rise above! @REVxMLJ #Faith #Inspiration

POST 2

🏗 Building a foundation for success requires determination and resilience. Just like Nehemiah, let your faith guide you to triumph over obstacles! @REVxMLJ #Determination #Resilience

POST 3

🤝 Collaboration and trust in God's favour bring remarkable success. Follow Nehemiah's example of unity to achieve greatness in your endeavours! @REVxMLJ #Teamwork #Unity

EPILOGUE

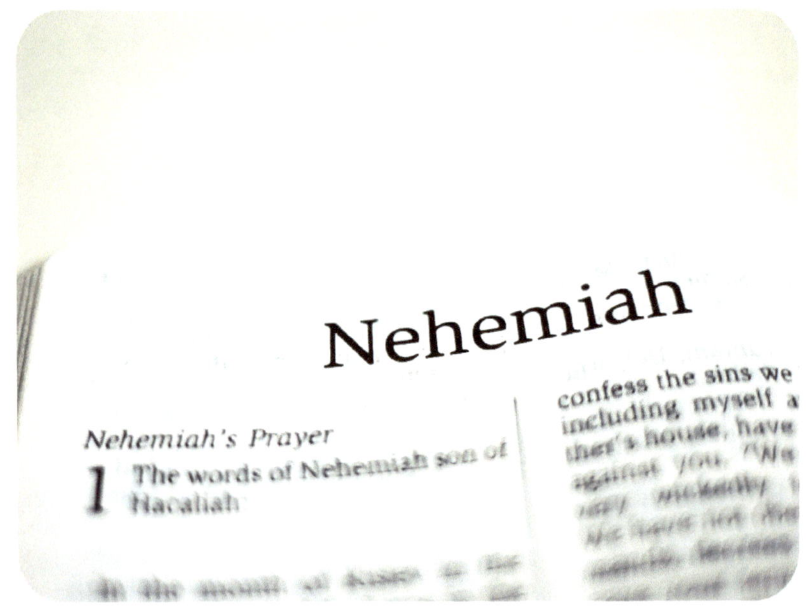

In this book, we have delved into Nehemiah's strategic approach, drawing valuable lessons for men and men who lead men. Throughout Nehemiah's journey, several key themes have emerged, teaching us profound insights that can transform our lives and leadership.

Firstly, Nehemiah's prayerful dependence on God serves as a poignant reminder of the need for men to seek divine guidance and wisdom in every aspect of life. His unwavering reliance on prayer demonstrates the power of connecting with God and seeking His will in all decisions.

Secondly, Nehemiah's strategic mindset is evident in his ability to assess the situation, formulate a plan, and execute it with precision. Men can learn from his careful planning and thoughtful approach, understanding the importance of strategy in tackling challenges and achieving goals.

Thirdly, Nehemiah exhibits visionary leadership by setting clear goals, rallying others to join the cause, and leading with integrity. His visionary mindset inspires men to know their purpose, cast a compelling vision, and guide others towards a shared objective.

Furthermore, Nehemiah's persistent diligence stands as a testament to the value of perseverance. Despite facing numerous challenges and opposition, he remained focused and determined. This tenacity encourages men to stay committed to their calling, put in the demanding work, and never give up.

Moreover, Nehemiah's emphasis on community restoration highlights the significance of investing in one's family, church, and local community. By prioritizing the rebuilding of Jerusalem's walls, he showcases the importance of nurturing strong relationships and creating a thriving environment that benefits all.

Nehemiah's remarkable success in completing the wall within a mere fifty-two days is a testament to his exceptional leadership, unwavering determination, and the favour of God. Men can draw inspiration from this achievement, understanding that with the right mindset and divine assistance, extraordinary accomplishments are possible.

As we conclude this journey through Nehemiah's strategic approach, let us embrace the powerful lessons learned. May we cultivate a prayerful dependence on God, adopt a strategic mindset, lead with vision and integrity, persistently pursue our goals, invest in our communities, and trust in the favour of God to guide us on our own remarkable journeys of transformation and leadership.

CONCLUDING PRAYER

Heavenly Father,

As we come to the end of this journey through Nehemiah's strategic approach, we thank you for the valuable lessons we have learned. We acknowledge our need for prayerful dependence on You, seeking Your guidance and wisdom in every aspect of our lives.

Teach us to trust in You wholeheartedly and recognize that our strength comes from You alone. Help us develop a strategic mindset, just as Nehemiah did. Grant us discernment to assess situations, formulate plans, and execute them with precision.

Fill our hearts with creativity and wisdom as we navigate the challenges of life and leadership. May we always prioritise your will in our decision-making.

Lord, inspire us to be visionary leaders. Grant us the courage to set clear goals, rally others towards a greater purpose, and lead with integrity.

Give us the humility to serve those entrusted to our care and guide them with love and compassion. May our leadership be a reflection of Your character and bring glory to Your Name.

In times of opposition and difficulty, empower us with persistent diligence. Teach us the value of perseverance and steadfastness in pursuing the task at hand.

When discouragement sets in, remind us to stay focussed on the ultimate goal and trust in Your faithfulness to see us through.

Lord, instil in us a desire to restore and nurture healthy communities around us. Help us invest in our families, churches, and local communities, making a positive impact in the lives of others.

May we be agents of unity, healing, and restoration, following Nehemiah's example.

Finally, Lord, we thank you for the extraordinary accomplishments that are possible when we align our lives and leadership with Your purposes.

Grant us the courage to dream big, knowing that with You on our side, nothing is impossible.

We commit ourselves anew to serving You faithfully and leading with honour and integrity. Continue to mold us into men who live out the principles we have learned, seeking to make a difference in the world around us. In Jesus' name, we pray. Amen.

NOTES

Write down six goals for your present and your future from the lessons learned in this study and in this manual and from the discussions with your band of brothers.

1.____

2.____

3.____

4.____

5.____

6.____

7.____

SOCIAL MEDIA INFORMATION